Family

I wonder what yours is like... large or small?

Write your own name in the middle figure. Write the names of your family in the figures around it – don't forget to include grandparents, aunts, uncles and cousins. (If there aren't enough figures draw some more yourself.)

My family

I wonder what your family are like as people. Are they bossy? friendly? good for playing games with? Do you ever argue?

It can be great fun discovering new things about members of your family; a secret about Mum when she was a girl, a story about Grandad as a boy. Why not try to discover something special about one person in your family?

Some families are very small; some are very large. Some families are happy most of the time, whilst others have more problems.

What's the best thing about your family?

(Write about or draw a picture of your discovery here.)

The human family

We all belong to our own family.

We also belong to the family of the human race.

See if you can discover the ten differences between the two pictures below.

Discovering about our family and about the human family can be great fun. But there is an even greater family to discover, and it is the very best family of all. It's God's forever family.

Spot the Difference!

Now that may have come as a surprise discovery. But it is fantastically true.

GOD, the one who made all of the vast universe;

the one who made the brilliant world in which we live;

God's family

the one who made you the fabulous person you are, has a family.

(Draw a picture of yourself in the box on the left.)

And he wants you, your family, your friends, in fact everybody, to be part of it forever.

Brilliant news or what?

God's world

God is responsible for making everything, and keeping it going. So it makes sense that he should want it all to be great. He loves the world he has made.

What is the best thing you have ever discovered about God's world?

Tick your favourite discovery, or if it is not shown then draw it for yourself.

Flowers

Trees

Animals

Friends

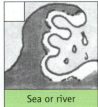
Sea or river

Music

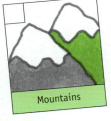
Mountains

What about Science's discoveries?
Scientists have discovered a lot about the way the world works. There are many ideas about how the world has been made but scientists cannot fully explain why we are here. Only God knows the complete answer to this question. He has told us in the Bible that he is responsible for making and keeping everything. He has also told us that human beings have a special responsibility to care for the world. This is something we have not been very good at doing.

God has told us that people are the very best thing in his creation. We are the best because God made us like himself. He made us to care for the world for him. We are made to be part of his family.

Made like God?
When the Bible tells us that we are made like God, it does not mean that we look like him. After all God does not have a body. But, like God, we can create things, love, feel, and make choices. Also, since we are like God, we are able to have a friendship with him.

But instead of living as part of God's family, people have always decided to do things their own way. It is as if we tell God that we know better than he does. We decide to lie sometimes, rather than always telling the truth. We choose to be unkind, even cruel, towards other people, rather than treating them lovingly.

We decide to misuse and pollute the world God has made, rather than care for it and use it responsibly. We make up our minds that we will be the boss of our own lives, rather than listen to God who made us.

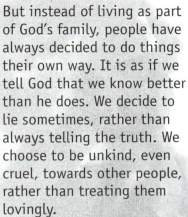

Being outside God's family

All of this is what the Bible calls sin. All of us think, speak and act in ways which show that we sin. We choose to go our own way. We decide to live outside of God's family.

But God still loves us and wants us to be part of the family.

God sends his Son Jesus to the world

God has shown us that he still loves us in many ways. The main way is by sending his Son, Jesus, to live in the world.

Jesus showed us what a human life without sin is like.

When we read about his life:

his birth...

...the way he treated people – children and grown ups, rich and poor...

...his teaching about God as our loving father...

...his power to heal sick people...

...and other miracles...

...his death...

...and his resurrection.

– we discover the most fantastic person who has ever lived.

What have you discovered about Jesus yourself?

....

....

Making discoveries is always exciting, isn't it?

Think about a time when you made an unexpected and exciting discovery. It might have been discovering a lost toy, or how to control a computer game. Or it might have been discovering a new friend, or finding out something special about a friend.

What was your discovery?

....

....

How did you feel about this discovery?

....

....

....

....

Discovering treasure

One story Jesus told was about someone making a wonderful discovery. Here it is:

"The kingdom of heaven is like what happens when someone finds treasure hidden in a field and buries it again. A person like that is happy and goes and sells everything in order to buy that field."

Jesus was saying that when we discover God's love for us, it is like discovering the most fantastic treasure we could ever possibly find.

Discovering that God made you and that he loves you is like finding a hidden treasure chest.

You may never have realised just how much God loves you. It is the most wonderful discovery you will ever make in your whole life.

But is it all too good to be true? More like the pot of gold at the end of a rainbow than a real treasure?

No! It is true. The way we know this may surprise you.

It is Jesus' death on the cross which is the greatest way God shows us his love.

Let me explain why.

Jesus died in our place

God knew that all the wrong things we do could not just be forgotten. They had to be dealt with. He knew too that we are not able to stop doing wrong things. However hard we try to do everything right, we always end up hurting others. Unkind words come out of our mouths. We let ourselves down. Even more importantly, we let God down.

So God did something to make it possible for him to forgive us so that we can join his family.

Jesus is the one person who has lived who has never let God down.

So he did not deserve to die at all, but God allowed Jesus' enemies to put him to death. They had him crucified. That is, he was nailed to a wooden cross and was left hanging there until he died.

When Jesus died, he was punished for all the wrong things we have ever done, thought and said. He died in our place.

Jesus died not simply to rescue us for the rest of this life, but so that we could be in God's family forever! What a discovery!

After his death, on a Friday, Jesus was buried by some friends. But when some other friends went to the grave early on the Sunday morning, they discovered that the grave was empty. Some angels told them Jesus

I'm sorry... I didn't mean to... I couldn't stop myself.

TRUE STORY

When a plane crashed into the frozen River Potomac in Washington, one survivor was seen helping others reach the rescue helicopter's winch. Each time the winch was lowered he helped another person onto the winch and they were lifted to safety. The final time the winch was lowered the man himself had died. He had died so that the others might have life.

FRIDAY

SUNDAY

was alive again. That day many people saw him alive on several occasions.

Over the next few weeks they saw him several times. He had risen from the dead. Jesus talked and ate with them, and allowed them to touch him. Then, once the disciples were sure he was alive for ever, he went back to heaven.

Jesus coming alive again shows us that God accepts Jesus' death as the way of bringing us into his family.

God's love is fantastic! We may have known about it for a while, or it may be we have just discovered it – like hidden treasure in a field.

When the person found the treasure they had to do something to make it their own. We need to do something to belong to God's family.

How to join God's family

1 The person had to give up something. So do we. We have to give up pretending we are good enough for God. We need to admit that we have made a mess of things.

We have to say sorry to God for thinking, saying and doing wrong things.

2 The person had to buy the field to make it their own. We do not have to buy anything but we do need to do something. We need to believe that Jesus died so that all those wrong things could be forgiven. We need to ask God to forgive us and welcome us into his family.

When we do this, we discover that he loves us so much that he forgives us completely. He makes us his child, a member of his family. He comes to be with us, by his Holy Spirit, to help us live as a member of his family from here on, forever. It's fantastic!

Some people find it hard to know what words to use to ask God to welcome them into his family. So here are some you might like to use. But you can use your own if you prefer.

Loving Father God this discovery is fantastic!
Thank you so much that you made me.
Thank you that you want me to be your child, one of your family.
I am really sorry for all the wrong things that I have thought, and said, and done.
Thank you that Jesus died on the cross so that I could be forgiven and be welcomed into your family.
Please forgive me now, and welcome me as your child.
I will need your help to live as one of your family, so please come and live in me by your Holy Spirit.
Help me to show others that I belong to your family.
I ask this in the name of Jesus Christ, your special Son.
Amen.

How to grow in God's family

Children start life in their family as a baby.

It is a bit like that for you now. You are like a new baby member of God's family. So you will need food and drink. You will need help. God as loving Father is with you by the Holy Spirit. God also gives you loads of older brothers and sisters in God's family to help as well.

Talk to one of them about how you can begin to grow as a child of God. Do it soon.

And, hey, welcome from me too. I have been in God's family now for over 25 years! My wife, Rosemary, and my four children (Caroline, David, Andrew and Sarah) are all part of God's family as well.

We live together in East London. Belonging to God's forever family is the most fantastic discovery we have ever made. It is the most fantastic one you can ever make as well.